UNICORN
coloring book
FOR KIDS

This Book
Belongs To :

Draw and color this unicorn

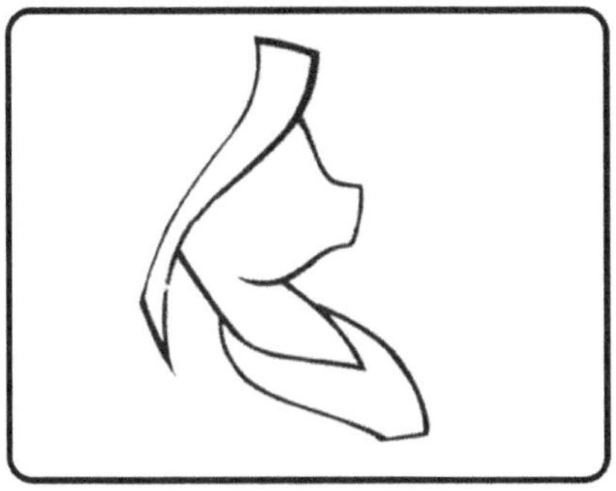

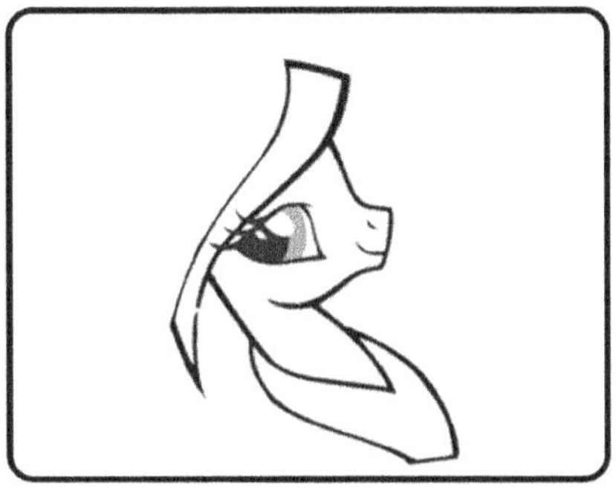

Step 1

Step 2

Step 3

Step 4

Step 5

Step 6

Draw and color this unicorn

Step 5

Step 6

Draw and color this unicorn

Step 1

Step 2

Step 3

Step 4

Step 5

Step 6

Draw and color this unicorn

Step 5

Step 6

Draw and color this unicorn

Step 5

Step 6

Draw and color this unicorn

Step 1

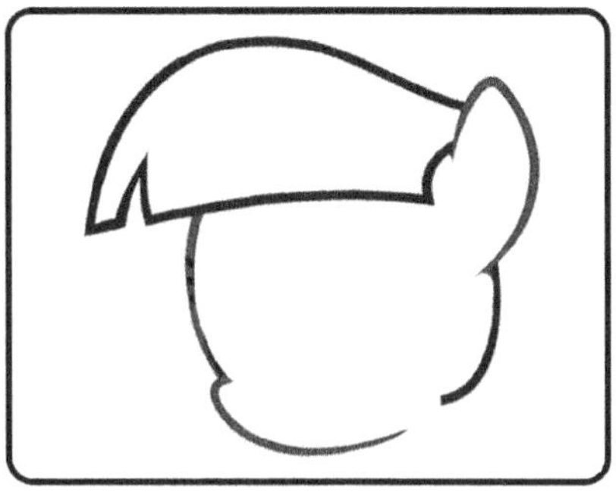

Step 2

Step 3

Step 4

Step 5

Step 6

Draw and color this unicorn

Step 5

Step 6

Draw and color this unicorn

Step 1

Step 2

Step 3

Step 4

Step 5

Step 6

Draw and color this unicorn

Step 5

Step 6

Draw and color this unicorn

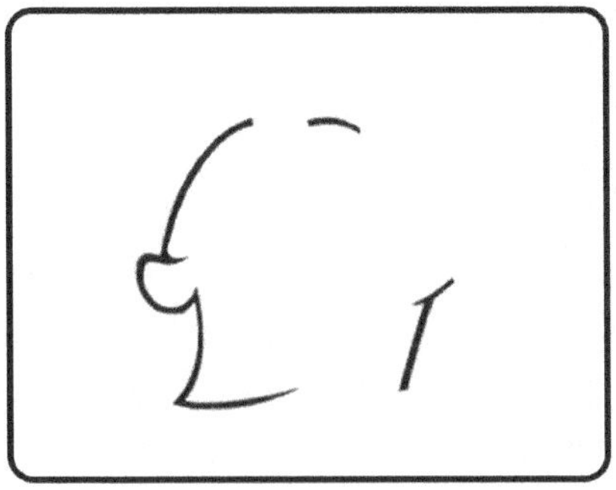

Step 1

Step 2

Step 3

Step 4

Step 5

Step 6

Draw and color this unicorn

Step 5

Step 6

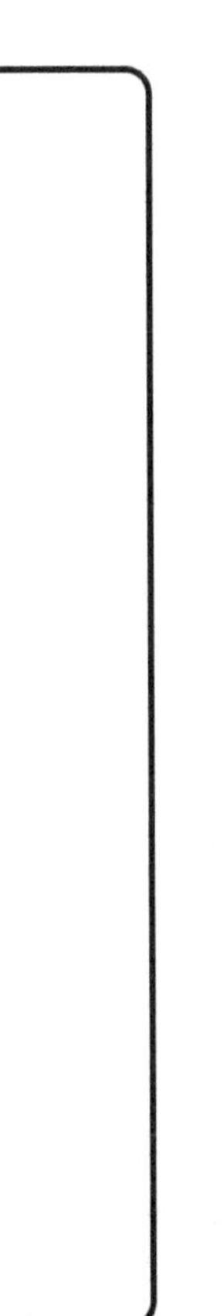

Draw and color this unicorn

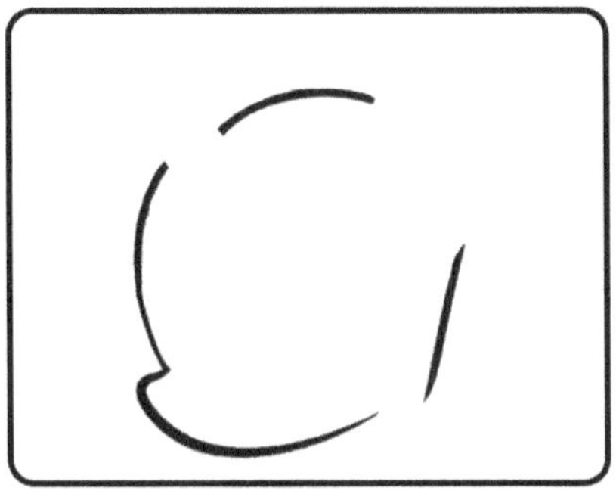

Step 1

Step 2

Step 3

Step 4

Step 5

Step 6

Draw and color this unicorn

Step 5

Step 6

Draw and color this unicorn

Step 1

Step 2

Step 3

Step 4

Step 5

Step 6

Draw and color this unicorn

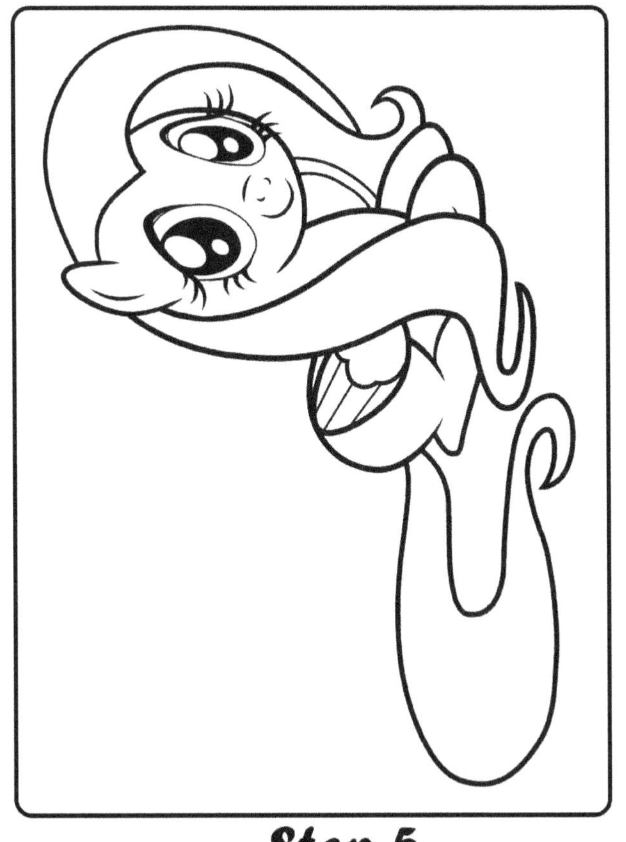

Step 5

Step 6

Draw and color this unicorn

Draw and color this unicorn

Step 5

**Step 6

Draw and color this unicorn

Step 1

Step 2

Step 3

Step 4

Step 5

Step 6

Draw and color this unicorn

Step 5

Step 6

Draw and color this unicorn

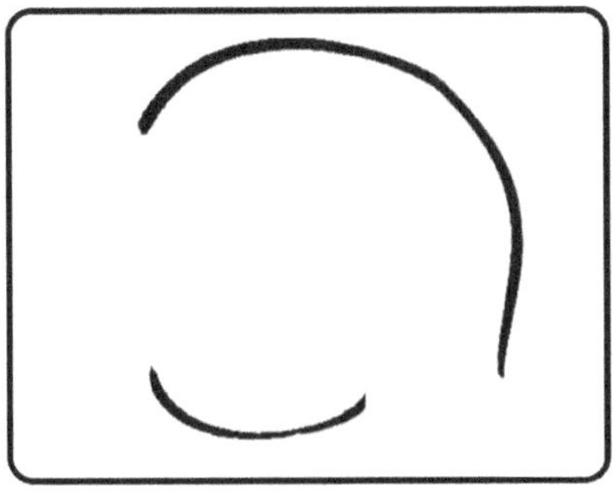

Step 1

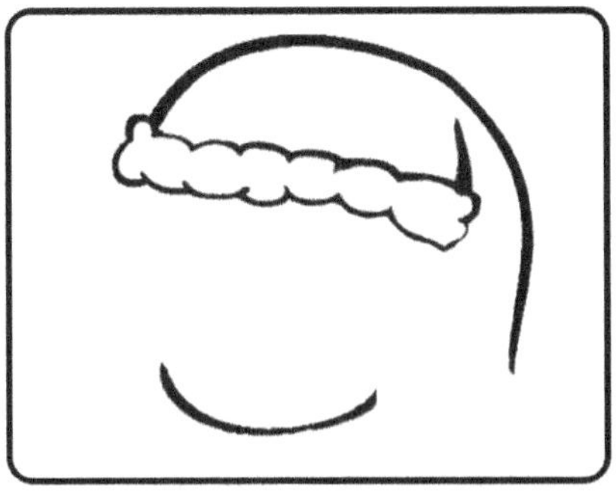

Step 2

Step 3

Step 4

Step 5

Step 6

Draw and color this unicorn

Step 5   **Step 6**

Draw and color this unicorn

Step 1

Step 2

Step 3

Step 4

Step 5

Step 6

Draw and color this unicorn

Step 5

Step 6

Draw and color this unicorn

Draw and color this unicorn

Step 5

Step 6